RRAAUUUUOOK

WHEEP
POP

BUOAK BUOAK
BA-GAWK

BURRRR

HOOT!

IEI-UO

MA-AH-AH

GEE-GEE

ROAUUUUUR!

HOW TO
CHAT
CHICKEN

**Gossip Gorilla, Babble Bee, Gab Gecko,
and Talk in 66 Other
Animal Languages**

**This book is dedicated to my parents
and, of course, to Sam.
– Nick**

What on Earth Books is an imprint of What on Earth Publishing
The Black Barn, Wickhurst Farm, Leigh, Tonbridge, Kent, UK, TN11 8PS
30 Ridge Road Unit B, Greenbelt, Maryland, 20770, United States

First published in the United States in 2023

Written by Dr. Nick Crumpton
Illustrated by Adrienne Barman
Designed by Daisy Symes

Staff for this book: Nancy Feresten, Publisher; Katy Lennon, Senior Editor; Andy Forshaw,
Art Director; Daisy Symes, Senior Designer; Lauren Fulbright, Production Manager.

Consultant: Paul Lawston, Learning Manager at WWT London Wetland Centre

With thanks to Dr. Kirsty Macleod.

Library of Congress Cataloging-in-Publication Data available upon request

ISBN: 9781804660430
RP/Haryana, India/05/2023
Printed in India
10 9 8 7 6 5 4 3 2 1

whatonearthbooks.com

HOW TO
CHAT
CHICKEN

Gossip Gorilla, Babble Bee, Gab Gecko, and Talk in 66 Other Animal Languages

By **Dr. Nick Crumpton**
Illustrated by **Adrienne Barman**

What on Earth Books

CONTENTS

NOISY NATURE

Have you ever wondered what your pet cat's meow means? Or what a firefly's flash is signaling? Well, maybe I can help...

I have been studying animals for many years, and during that time have come across some really amazing animal communication styles. In this book, I've collected some of my favorites, from hissing caterpillars to grunting gorillas and purring cats.

Animals communicate for lots of different reasons: sometimes to ask for food or make friends and other times to defend their territory or find a mate. Animals don't talk with words in the same way humans do. But they do often use sounds, movements, or smells to get their point across.

Join me on a journey through the animal kingdom and learn how to chat chicken, gossip with goats, and have discussions with dogs. On each page, I've listed some of the coolest animal noises that I've come across, along with their translation. Why not try them out for yourself as you go, to really get in touch with your wild side? I have also translated some of the other moving and shaking ways that animals communicate. Because sometimes it's not *what* you say, but *how* you say it!

Dr Nick

PRATTLING
with
PRIMATES

Humans sure are a noisy bunch of primates, but we're not the only ones! Our closest living relatives are great talkers, too...

CHIMPANZEES

Chimpanzees are found in Africa and are humans' closest living relatives. We have learned to understand some of the sounds that they use to communicate—however their behavior can be unpredictable...

HUU HU HUU
(What's that?)

This quiet whimper is made by chimps when they are investigating something new.

HE EH EU EH EH
(That tickles!)

Chimps laugh just like humans when they're playing with their friends.

KOAUU
(Stay back)

Coughs are usually meant as threats.

HU-OO HU OO HU-OO HU-OO HU-AA HU-AA
(I'm excited!)

The "pant-hoot" is very common and is made whenever something exciting happens in the troop. Make sure you breathe in on the "hu" and out on the "oo"s and "aa"s, getting faster and louder as you go!

MORE CHIMPANZEES

Chimpanzees are clever creatures. Not only do they use their voices to send signals to each other, they also use their surroundings.

THUM-DUM-DUM
(We're here... and we're dangerous!)

When a chimp hits its feet against the base of a tree, it creates a loud, low noise. This sound can carry for miles to distant groups of other chimps.

When chimpanzees feel threatened, they will often smack the gound to make low noises. They also make high-pitched screaming sounds.

THUMP!
(Stay BACK!)

SHK-SHK-SHAKE-SHAKE
(See—I'm dangerous!)

Aggressive noises are often accompanied by the rattling of trees to add an extra element of scariness.

GORILLAS

These great apes live in Africa in small groups. Each group is protected by a large silverback male. Gorillas are known for being gentle and can show some human-like emotions. However, males can get angry when challenged, so don't get on their bad side!

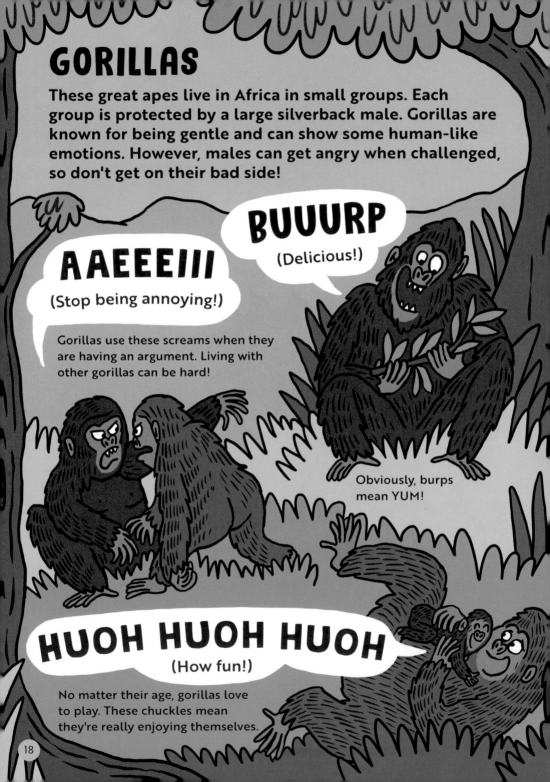

BUUURP
(Delicious!)

AAEEEIII
(Stop being annoying!)

Gorillas use these screams when they are having an argument. Living with other gorillas can be hard!

Obviously, burps mean YUM!

HUOH HUOH HUOH
(How fun!)

No matter their age, gorillas love to play. These chuckles mean they're really enjoying themselves.

GRNNNT
(I'm in charge)

Small grunts are made by silverback gorillas to keep the rest of their group in line.

HOOT!
(There's a problem—let's stick together.)

ROAUUUUUR!
(Get off my turf!)

It doesn't happen very often, but sometimes these low roars can be heard throughout the forest when males are fighting. There might also be the thud-thud-thud sound of the male beating his chest.

ORANGUTANS

There are three species (or types) of these rust-colored great apes. They live in the remaining forests of Sumatra and Borneo in Southeast Asia. Orangutans are very intelligent and also very loud! Some of their calls can be heard more than 1 mile (1.5 kilometers) away.

WHUUU-WHUUU-WHUUU...
(Hellooooo...)

"Long calls" can last for many minutes and are a way for orangutans to communicate with each other over large distances.

PCTHTHUTHUTHTU
(I'm working on my nest.)

A raspberry might sound rude, but it can just mean that the orangutan is busy and wants to be left alone.

AEEEEIIII
(Go away!)

Screaming means "leave me alone!"

MUUUUUAAAA
(Oh good, you're back!)

NIGHT MONKEYS

The jungles of South America can be noisy at nighttime. If you feel like having a midnight chat with some night monkeys, you might need to warm up your vocal cords to prepare for some shrieking, gulping, and sneezing...

GLP!
(Hey!)

Night monkeys
make a gulping
noise when they
see each other.

H-RUUUUM
(Who are you?)

This low grunt
is made when
a night monkey
meets a stranger.

CHOO!
(Stay back!)

A sneeze-like sound
is used to intimidate
other night monkeys.

COMMON MARMOSETS

These South American primates are smaller than cats. They live in troops among the trees in the Brazilian jungle. The calls of these little creatures can be mistaken for that of a bird, so you have to listen closely!

TSEE TSEE!
(Get lost!)

SQUEEEII
(Sorry—I didn't mean to get in your way!)

PHEE...?
(Are you there?)

This sweet, soft call is used to contact other marmosets when they can't see each other.

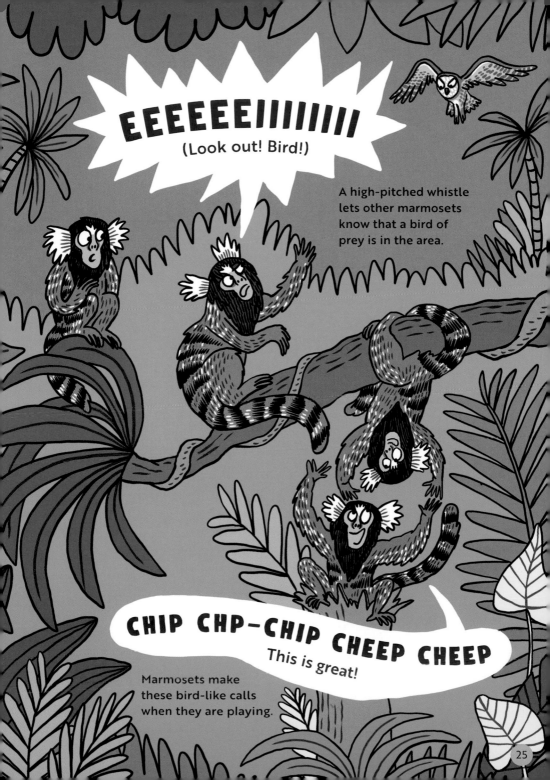

EEEEEEIIIIIIII
(Look out! Bird!)

A high-pitched whistle lets other marmosets know that a bird of prey is in the area.

CHIP CHP-CHIP CHEEP CHEEP
This is great!

Marmosets make these bird-like calls when they are playing.

NOISY NEIGHBORS

We share our world with millions of other types of animals, and we even invite some into our homes and gardens. So it would be rude not to try to understand what our friendly neighborhood animals are saying!

CHICKENS

You might have heard hens go "boouuuaaaak" and roosters go "eaaurg kegh-ahhh oo-OOOO!" But there are lots of other sounds that are useful to learn if you want to chat chicken.

KAAAH!
(Danger in the sky!)

The top chicken, or rooster, alerts everyone else to watch out if they spy danger. The sound can change depending on where the danger is.

PURRRRRR
(I'm happy.)

When chickens are comfortable and feel safe, they purr or murmur. Mother hens also use this sound to call their chicks.

WHEE WHEE WHEE!
(This is tasty!)

This sound is made by chicks when they are feeding. It means they're enjoying their food.

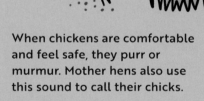

BUOK BUOK BUK BUKBUKBUBKBK
(Danger on the ground!)

BUOAK, BUOAK, BA-GAWK
(Move please, I need that nest!)

There are only so many spots in which to lay an egg, so sometimes hens need to share. However, they're not always happy about it!

GGGGGRRRRRRRRRR
(Get away from me and my eggs!)

DOGS

Dogs' ancestors were wolves that hunted in packs and made noises to stay in contact with one another. Today, our pet pooches still make many of the same noises to communicate with each other, and with us!

OOOUUUUUUUU
(Hello!)

GRRRRRRRRR
(Stay back!)

HINNNNNNNN!
(I'm so excited!)

HMMM! (This is fun!)

AROHOOOOOO! (This is super interesting!)

UUUWL!

Shiba inus can make a high-pitched scream when they are frustrated or overexcited.

Be careful if a dog shows its teeth.

RRRRARFF ARFF! (You don't belong here!)

Barks can mean many different things. They also sound different depending on which breed is making the noise. A low bark is usually a sign that the dog is angry.

TALKING WITH SMELLS

Some animals use special types of chemicals called pheromones to communicate. Pheromones are given off by organs in an animal's body, or in their pee or poop. They can be used to attract mates, mark territory, or find prey.

Pheromones give out information about an animal. They can tell others whether it is male or female or what type of animal it is. Animals such as dogs will spray their pheromones onto surfaces, such as lampposts, so that other dogs will know that they have been there. Lampposts can become like doggy chat rooms with lots of different pheromones from lots of different dogs.

Animals can detect pheromones using a special organ inside their nose or mouth. Pheromones can also be sniffed directly from the animals' scent glands. A dog's scent glands are right next to its bottom, which is why dogs will always sniff each other's bottoms!

CATS

Cats may have first started to live with humans about 12,000 years ago. Since then, they have become one of the most popular pets in the world. Cats sleep for about 15 hours a day, but when they're not snoozing, they can have lots to say.

HAIIIIIISSSSSHHH
(Get away from me!)

IRRUP-IRRUP
(Come on!)

Cats often use chirrups or trills to talk to their kittens. These noises can also mean that they are excited about something—like receiving a treat!

KA. AH. ARRA. KAH...
(I want to eat that...)

Cats will usually only chatter when they are watching birds.

KRRRKRRRKRRRKRRRKRRRKRRR
(This is comfy.)

Kittens meow to get their mother's attention. As grown-ups, cats meow to ask their owners to play with them or feed them.

MEIOOW
(Hey! I'm right here.)

Purring usually means that a cat is comfortable. Sometimes a cat will also knead a blanket, or something soft, to help soothe itself.

PIGS

Pigs and their relatives, such as wild hogs, peccaries, and babirusas, are very social and intelligent animals. They make nasal, throaty calls to stay in contact with other pigs.

HNGFF

(Everything is A-okay!)

Pigs grunt to let other pigs know that they are there and everything's okay. They normally make this noise as they are going about their daily business.

GGGFF
(This is relaxing.)

A longer grunt is similar to a cat's purr and means they are relaxed. Female pigs make this noise when they are suckling their piglets.

OUURF OUURF
(What was that?)

Pigs often bark when they're playing or when they are startled.

HORSES

Horses often communicate using their bodies and ears. But they can also be very talkative. If you want to have a chat with a stallion, here are a few phrases that might come in useful.

NEEEIGHEHEIHEI!

(What's that weird thing?)

This horsey noise is probably the most famous. It can mean that a horse is excited to see you or that it has seen something that worries it.

A short blast of air through the nose usually means that the horse is a bit unsure of something.

SNORT

(Hmm... I'm not so sure about this.)

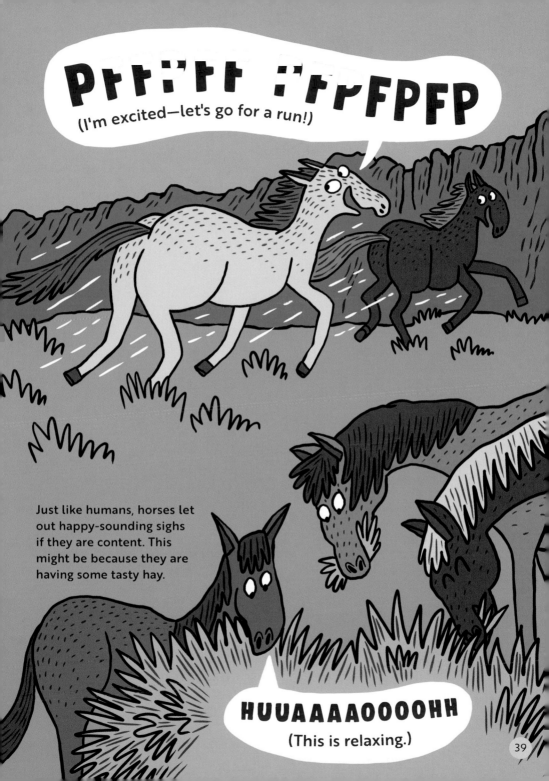

Just like humans, horses let out happy-sounding sighs if they are content. This might be because they are having some tasty hay.

39

GOATS

Humans can gather information from the words that they use when they talk. But they can also get extra information about how someone might be feeling from *how* they are talking. Amazingly, this is something that humans and goats have in common!

Goats can recognize the differences in other goats' bleats (even if they might sound the same to humans). To test this, scientists played the sounds of happy goats enjoying a tasty treat to some other goats. They found that the listening goats had increased heart rates. When they heard the sounds made by sad goats (who were recorded when they weren't allowed food) their heart rates stayed normal.

For a long time scientists thought that being able to read the emotions of other animals was something that only primates and a few other animals could do. To find this ability in goats was quite a surprise! So maybe think twice next time you gossip with a goat—they just might be understanding more than you think!

MU-U-AH-AH-AH
(Look at me!)

BABBLING BUGS

Bugs are insects, spiders, worms, snails, centipedes, and all manner of other invertebrates (creatures without a backbone). You may think that they are pretty quiet, apart from the occasional buzz of a fly. But that's not always true...

BEES

Bees are well known for the buzzing sound that they make. The sound is made by their wings, which can beat up to 230 times per second! Bees also have a few other ways of communicating—they make noises and some of them also dance!

Honeybees make hissing sounds when their hives are rocked or damaged. This might be by an animal such as a honey badger trying to steal some honey.

HSSS
(Stop doing that!)

PP-PP
(I'm the queen here!)

Queen bees make short, pipping sounds that seem to keep younger queens away and stop them from taking over the hive.

BUZZZZZ
(This is how you find the flowers...)

One dance that bees do is called the waggle dance. It tells other bees where to find flowers and nectar. How far the bee dances as it walks gives the flowers' position in relation to the Sun.

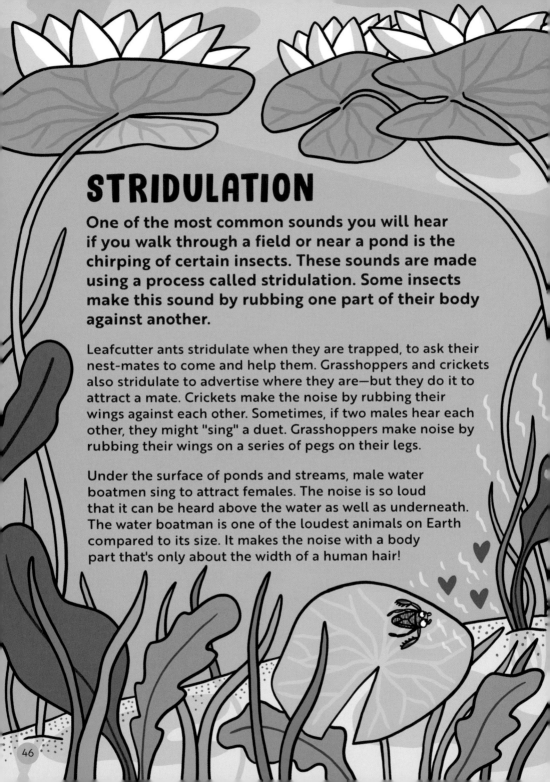

STRIDULATION

One of the most common sounds you will hear if you walk through a field or near a pond is the chirping of certain insects. These sounds are made using a process called stridulation. Some insects make this sound by rubbing one part of their body against another.

Leafcutter ants stridulate when they are trapped, to ask their nest-mates to come and help them. Grasshoppers and crickets also stridulate to advertise where they are—but they do it to attract a mate. Crickets make the noise by rubbing their wings against each other. Sometimes, if two males hear each other, they might "sing" a duet. Grasshoppers make noise by rubbing their wings on a series of pegs on their legs.

Under the surface of ponds and streams, male water boatmen sing to attract females. The noise is so loud that it can be heard above the water as well as underneath. The water boatman is one of the loudest animals on Earth compared to its size. It makes the noise with a body part that's only about the width of a human hair!

CHIRP!

(Come hang out with me!)

NESSUS SPHINX HAWK MOTH CATERPILLARS

Caterpillars can easily be picked off leaves and eaten by predators, such as birds. They handle this problem in different ways. Some caterpillars are poisonous. Others are excellent at hiding. Scientists have discovered that one caterpillar—the Nessus sphinx hawk moth caterpillar—can "scream" to warn off anything that is trying to nibble at it.

This scream-like noise is made by the caterpillar moving air back and forth out of its mouth and throat, a little like a person snoring. The first part of their scream sounds like a hiss as they breathe air in, and then a "kk-kk-kk" sound follows as the air is pushed out.

Other insects make sounds by pushing air out of tubes on the sides of their bodies (like the Madagascar hissing cockroach). But this caterpillar is one of the only soft-bodied bugs known to communicate with sounds made by moving air through its mouth.

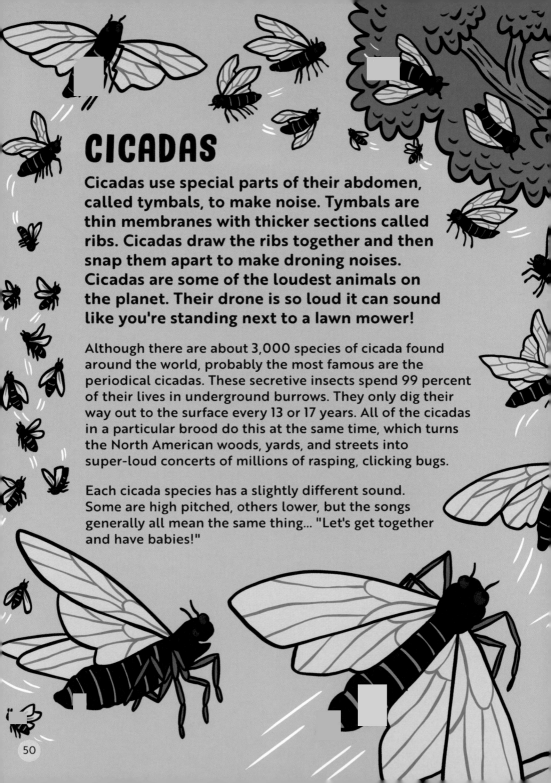

CICADAS

Cicadas use special parts of their abdomen, called tymbals, to make noise. Tymbals are thin membranes with thicker sections called ribs. Cicadas draw the ribs together and then snap them apart to make droning noises. Cicadas are some of the loudest animals on the planet. Their drone is so loud it can sound like you're standing next to a lawn mower!

Although there are about 3,000 species of cicada found around the world, probably the most famous are the periodical cicadas. These secretive insects spend 99 percent of their lives in underground burrows. They only dig their way out to the surface every 13 or 17 years. All of the cicadas in a particular brood do this at the same time, which turns the North American woods, yards, and streets into super-loud concerts of millions of rasping, clicking bugs.

Each cicada species has a slightly different sound. Some are high pitched, others lower, but the songs generally all mean the same thing... "Let's get together and have babies!"

GOOD VIBRATIONS

Sounds are vibrations. Many animals talk to each other by making vibrations that travel through the air or water. But some critters make noise by vibrating objects. Here are a few that you might be able to detect by putting your ear to the ground.

Banner-tailed kangaroo rats speak to each other using squeaks, squeals, growls, and chuckles. They also communicate by drumming their feet on the floor. Kangaroo rats are quite territorial and their taps warn other kangaroo rats to stay away from their burrows.

The Puerto Rican white-lipped frog thumps the ground with its vocal pouch every time it calls. This helps the sound travel farther—through the ground as well as the air.

Male wolf spiders vibrate their bodies to get in touch with females. They will often stand on dried leaves so the leaves vibrate, too. This makes their signals travel farther by moving from leaf to leaf. If the vibration reaches a female wolf spider then, bingo! Message received!

FIREFLIES

Fireflies are nocturnal, which means they are awake at nighttime and asleep during the day. When it's dark, it can be tricky to see. But fireflies have a clever solution—they make their own light.

There are more than 2,000 species of fireflies that can be found from the plains of North America to the forests of Malaysia. Despite their name, they are actually not flies, but a variety of beetle. Almost all fireflies produce light from the tips of their abdomens. Their bodies do this by combining chemicals with oxygen. Males use this flashing to get the attention of females.

But the flashing can have another use. Some female fireflies flash to lure other kinds of beetles to them. When a beetle moves toward the light, the firefly eats it!

Most fireflies flash on their own, but some tropical species flash in sync with one another. When the males all flash at the same time at dusk, they can create huge, tree-sized light shows.

COMMOTION
in the
OCEAN

The seas, rivers, and waterways of Earth can seem like tranquil, quiet places. But in reality, they are busy, bustling worlds full of animals trying to communicate with each other. Let's dive into what some of these watery wordsmiths are trying to say.

DOLPHINS

Atlantic bottlenose dolphins are complex communicators. Each dolphin has a unique whistle, which acts as its name. They also use touch and other gestures, such as nods, to interact with one another.

SLAP
(I'm peeved!)

If a dolphin slaps the water with its tail, it could mean that it's annoyed or that it's trying to get another dolphin's attention. Tail slaps produce shock waves and can also be used to stun fish, making them easier to catch.

PUUUUOOOOOF!
(This is exciting!)

When it's having fun, an Atlantic bottlenose dolphin blows air loudly out of its blowhole.

HOW DO BABY ANIMALS LEARN TO TALK?

When human babies are learning to talk, they make the same sounds over and over again—like "ma-ma-ma-ma" or "ba-ba-ba-ba." This "babbling" helps them understand the noises their mouths can make. Biologists have recently discovered that very chatty animals also babble when they're learning to talk.

Baby bottlenose dolphins make lots of random noises when they're learning how to talk. They need to learn all of the clicks and squeaks that they will depend on for communication when they grow up.

Bats use very complicated sounds to communicate with each other. The greater sac-winged bat sings in a similar way to birds and uses noises to echolocate and find prey. To practice these sounds, pups make the same noises over and over again in their roosts.

Baby birds also have to slowly learn how to make sounds. Zebra finches and Bengalese finches learn songs in the same way human babies do. They copy their parents and they practice!

HUMPBACK WHALES

Baleen whales are the pop stars of the ocean. Several kinds are known to sing to each other: minke whales, fin whales, blue whales, and—most famously—humpback whales.

Humpback whales are masters of underwater concerts—and if you don't like their songs, tough luck! They are so loud that they can be heard 2.5 miles (4 kilometers) away!

Humpback whale songs use very low notes that sound like groans and incredibly high notes that sound like screeches. Their songs can last for 30 minutes or more and be very complicated. Humpback whales also repeat songs in sessions, like concerts, that can last all day.

Humpback whales learn each other's songs but also mix them up, singing certain parts for longer and cutting out other sections. Very quickly, these songs change and become slightly different versions of the original song.

We don't know for sure why humpback whales sing, but we do know that it's only the males that do it. Some scientists believe the songs help the males to find a mate.

ELEPHANT SEALS

Near the chilly oceans of Antarctica live the gigantic southern elephant seals. Don't let their peculiar noses fool you, these are some of the most dangerous and aggressive mammals on Earth. And that nose is a pretty incredible instrument for making some fascinating noises!

HHAI! HHAI!
(Where's my baby?)

Elephant seal moms use this noise to call for their pups when they come ashore after fishing.

ROO-UH-
(I'm the SCARIEST!)

This nasal roar means trouble's afoot. This sound is made by males when they are challenging each other for the females. It means "if you don't back down, there's going to be trouble!"

CRABS AND LOBSTERS

Crustaceans, such as crabs and lobsters, can be quite chatty if you know what to listen for. They don't speak to each other using their voices—instead, they make "cracking" sounds.

Spiny lobsters can stridulate in the same way that some insects do. They make rattling noises by moving their antennae against a part of their head. Unusually for the animal kingdom, it is mostly the females that make this sound to attract males to mate with.

Other crustaceans, such as fiddler crabs, can make deafening CRACKs by snapping their claws. These noises are probably made to scare other creatures away from their territory.

Some crabs can also communicate with each other in a quieter way—by waving. Hermit crabs raise one of their legs in order to show they're up for a fight.

Wanna fight?

FROGS

If you ever find yourself near a pond, you might be lucky enough to hear a frog. The typical sound that we think of with frogs is "ribbit," but many frogs don't make that noise at all!

American bullfrogs make a grating "grau-g-g-gga" noise, and the midwife toad makes soft, high-pitched "be-bi-boop-be" sounds. These different calls are their way of telling each other what type of frog they are. That way they know who is nearby and don't waste energy talking to frogs from a different species.

Frogs can make a whole range of sounds. The most common frog calls are love songs—made by males to attract females. But frogs also make "release" calls when they're receiving unwanted attention and want to be left alone. Some can even scream when they are attacked by predators.

WRUAAAAAK-WROOOOOOWK
(I'm an Indian Bullfrog!)

MORE FROGS

Some frogs use gestures as well as sounds to communicate. This is especially useful when they live in noisy places.

The glass frog *Sachatamia orejuela* lives right next to waterfalls in Ecuador and Colombia. Rather than competing with the roaring water, these frogs wave their large hands to "call" to each other.

Brazilian torrent frogs also use their bodies as well as their voices to attract females. They often sing sweetly using a mix of peeps and squeaks, but they will also tremble their feet, waggle their toes, and stretch their legs. They will even lift and wave their arms and bob their heads up and down and from side to side. They put on quite a show!

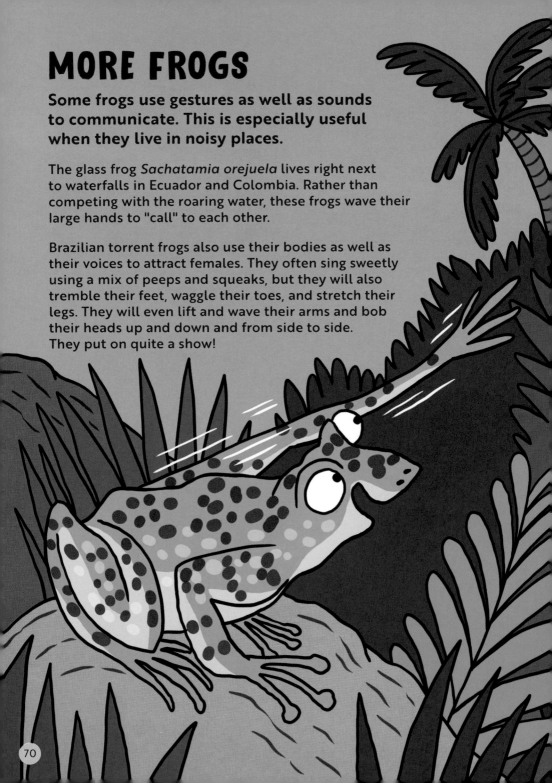

IEI-UO
(Hi Mom!)

This cute squeak is made by a gator baby calling to its mom. They even start making it while still inside their eggs.

HHRRRRRR
(I'm *THIS* big!)

ALLIGATORS

Reptiles aren't the chattiest of animals. But if you come face to toothy snout with an American alligator, it might be wise to have these phrases handy.

HHHUSSSSS
(Get away from my babies!)

If you hear this hiss, look for the nearest tree and run...

UMMMBLE

HHHUSSSSS
(You don't scare me!)

You might *see* this noise as well as *hear* it. Male alligators make these loud, deep rumbles by vibrating their bodies. This makes the water splash and dance off their backs.

FISH

You might not think of fish as being too chatty. But schools of fish can make a real racket! Here are some of the noisiest fish from around the world.

BURRR
(You're cute!)

Croaking gourami fish are very social. They use frog-like sounds to attract potential mates.

THUUMMP
(Let's give each other room.)

If there are lots of blotcheye soldierfish in one place, it can be tricky to find food. So they make this sound to ask their friends for a bit of space.

KNOCK-KNOCK-KNOCK
(Let's rumble.)

Blacktail shiners make knocking noises to scare off their rivals.

Sometimes, Atlantic cod make a grunting sound at the end of arguments.

GRRRRRUNT
(Beat it!)

I don't want any trouble...

Clownfish back down from fights by shaking their heads quickly.

CUTTLEFISH

These elegant creatures are related to squid and octopuses, and there are more than 120 different species of them. They can control cells in their skin to change their color, pattern, and texture in order to disguise themselves and communicate.

I AM SCARY!

When threatened, a cuttlefish might stretch up its tentacles to make itself look bigger.

If a cuttlefish needs to make a speedy escape from a predator, it can squirt a cloud of ink into the water. This acts as a distraction so that the cuttlefish can escape.

YOU ARE FEELING VERY SLEEPY...

Cuttlefish perform hypnotic displays where stripes of color move across their skin. This can mesmerize their prey and make them easier to catch with their super stretchy tentacles.

WILD WORDS

From the tops of the highest mountains to the ground beneath our feet, wild animals are everywhere. And they create a real hubbub with all their chatting!

GIANT PANDAS

Giant pandas might look cuddly, but they are actually solitary creatures that prefer to be left alone. Mothers and babies talk to one another, though. And so do adults looking for a mate. Giant pandas are found in the forests of southwest China.

BHA-UHAHUHAUHAUHAUU
(You look nice.)

Male pandas make bleating noises to attract a mate. These noises are similar to the sounds made by sheep.

CHRP CHIRP CHIP
(Oh... thank you very much!)

Females respond with chirps if they are interested.

SNOW LEOPARDS

High up in the mountains of central Asia there are a number of sounds you should listen for. If you hear any of these, you might be close to one of the rarest big cats in the world—the snow leopard. And you should also be very wary. You don't want to be taken for a Himalayan blue sheep—this cat's favorite food!

GRRRRRORRORORORRRR
(I'm angry.)

As with other cats, big or small, growls can be signs of annoyance or of feeling threatened.

HU-HUH-HUH
(I'm comfy.)

Tigers, jaguars, and snow leopards can't purr because of the shape of their throats. But blowing air through their nose, making a "huff" sound, can mean a similar thing.

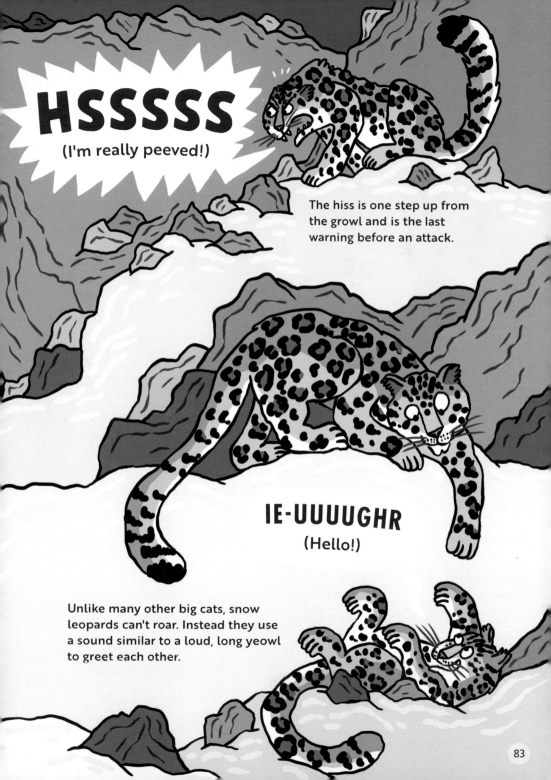

HSSSSS
(I'm really peeved!)

The hiss is one step up from the growl and is the last warning before an attack.

IE-UUUUGHR
(Hello!)

Unlike many other big cats, snow leopards can't roar. Instead they use a sound similar to a loud, long yeowl to greet each other.

HIPPOPOTAMUSES

You can find hippopotamuses bathing in the rivers and lakes of Africa. They tend to look relaxed most of the time, but if you get close enough to talk to one, you might need to watch out...

PPFFFFFT
(I'm not sure I like you. Stay away.)

HOOOOAAAAANNNK
(Hey! Seriously, stay out.)

Hippos often stay hidden in the water and reeds. They make a rumbly grunt to let other hippos know to stay away.

RRRRAAAUUUUUUUUOOK
(This is my turf—get lost!)

Everybody! This is my turf! SEE!

By twirling their tails while pooping, hippos spread their poop everywhere. They're trying to say that whatever their poop lands on, belongs to them.

I'm serious!

This open-mouthed threat means if it continues to be bothered, a hippo will soon start a fight.

MEERKATS

Meerkats are incredibly social. They have different warnings for different predators and can even let others know how close the danger is. While basking in the sun in the Kalahari desert in Africa, meerkats talk to each other, taking turns speaking.

WHUP–WHUP–WHUP
(Uuuh. I think that's a jackal in the distance...)

WHUUGH–WHUUGH
(Argh! Yes! It's definitely a jackal!)

PRAIRIE DOGS

These herbivorous rodents live in large groups, or "towns," on the Great Plains of North America. Prairie dogs have many predators, so they always need to be on the lookout for incoming danger. If a predator is spotted, they will raise the alarm, using one of these calls.

PEEP-PEEP-PEEP

(Coyote!)

UUOUK-KE-UHKE-UHKE-UHKE-UHKE-UHKE

(This is our turf!)

You can use a dog's chew toy to help you make this series of fast, squeaky calls. (I wouldn't recommend putting it in your mouth though!)

EEUP-EEUP-EEUP
(Yikes! Humans!)

Prairie dogs have another call that sounds lower than their alarm for coyotes. It means they have spotted a particular species of talking ape!

CHIP!
(This way, kids!)

This quieter sound helps moms show their kids where to go.

AFRICAN ELEPHANTS

African savanna elephants live in extended family groups led by a powerful female. Family members look out for each other, especially the little ones. They are the world's biggest land animals and have very powerful voices, so get ready to SHOUT!

ROOOOOO
(Stay away!)

BWWAAAAAIIIIIIIII
(Get away!)

A trumpet blast means that the elephant is angry and will attack if it needs to.

PAARUUUP
(This is so much fun!)

But not all trumpets are loud. Young elephants make these quieter sounds when they're playing.

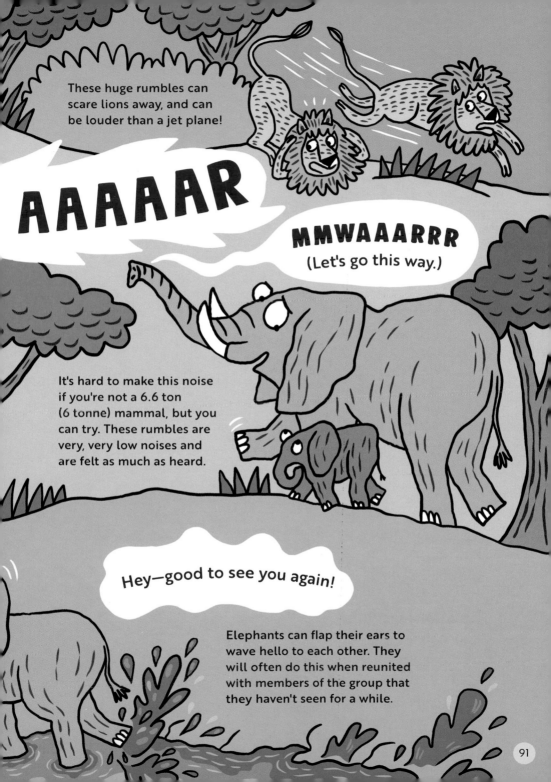

These huge rumbles can scare lions away, and can be louder than a jet plane!

AAAAAR

MMWAAARRR
(Let's go this way.)

It's hard to make this noise if you're not a 6.6 ton (6 tonne) mammal, but you can try. These rumbles are very, very low noises and are felt as much as heard.

Hey—good to see you again!

Elephants can flap their ears to wave hello to each other. They will often do this when reunited with members of the group that they haven't seen for a while.

NAKED MOLE RATS

A dialect is a form of language that people from a certain area use. For example, in the UK people call purple, pear-shaped vegetables "aubergines," while in the U.S., people call these "eggplants."

It seems some species of animals also have dialects depending on where they live. Naked mole rats are super-social rodents. They live in colonies ruled by a queen, in a similar way to how bees live. They talk to each other with squeaks and clicks, which sound slightly different depending on which colony they are from. If a mole rat squeaks with a different sound—it might be an invader from a rival gang!

WHOO-WHOO
(Helloooo!)

FOXES

Fox calls are one of the most widely spoken languages in the animal kingdom. Foxes are found on every continent except Antarctica, so this is a must-know language for nocturnal globetrotters.

ACK-ACK-A-ACK-ACK-A
(This is my yard!)

You don't want to hang around if you hear this. It means the fox is angry and might get aggressive!

MEUW
(You're the boss!)

A handy phrase when you need to try to calm a fox down!

GECKOS

Geckos are very chatty reptiles and are superstars at pest control. They usually spend their evenings gobbling up thousands of tasty insects, jabbering away with each other as they do!

TRILLLLL
(Leave me alone!)

If the New Caledonian giant gecko makes this loud noise that lasts for a few seconds it might be in distress.

CHIRP
(Hey!)

These small noises are the closest noise male geckos have to barking. They are used to warn other males to stay away or to attract females.

CLICK
(I like you!)

Mediterranean house geckos make clicking noises to attract mates.

CLICK
(I'm a cricket!)

The turnip-tailed gecko might also make these noises to sound like insects it wants to catch.

TASMANIAN DEVILS

Tasmanian devils are very territorial creatures that are only found in the wild on the Australian island of Tasmania. These feisty mammals will angrily defend their hunting grounds from intruders. Their noises are usually growls, grumbles, and shrieks, so get ready to be loud and fearless!

HUUFFF

(Hey—we should hang out.)

Males make this huffing noise when approaching female devils.

Tasmanian devils make this clicking sound as a threat.

WILD on the WING

Birds are some of the most impressive singers, talkers, and show-offs in the animal kingdom. But it's not just birds that can fly. Look out for the only mammal that can flap its wings and use its voice in amazing ways, too.

CROWS

Crows are some of the most intelligent birds in the world. They have lots of sounds that they can use to communicate. They love to chatter, so here are a few phrases to listen for.

RATGATGATGATGATGA
(Look out!)

The fast crow "rattle" seems to be made only by females. They use it to alert their family to something, such as an incoming threat.

CAW-CAW
(I'm calling in the troops!)

This call is asking for back-up when defending territory.

HOU-HOUEEE
(I'm hungry!)

C-HOOO
(Don't worry, I'm coming!)

Adults use this cooing noise to calm younger crows down. This is especially useful if they've been waiting for food!

GABURAHGARAGLLE
(Babble, babble.)

Like humans babies, crow chicks babble to themselves to figure out how to make different noises.

KHO!
(Hey, everyone, come here!)

The short "kho" is used to assemble members of the family together.

BATS

Bats are a different type of flying creature. They are not birds, but mammals—and the only mammals that can fly. Bats have very clever ways of making noise to communicate and also to see!

Like dolphins, bats are able to echolocate. This means they make high-pitched squeaks then use the echoes that bounce back to create a mental picture of the world around them. Echolocation gives them the ability to "see" in complete darkness.

There are more than 1,000 species of bat, and they each use different sounds. A lot of their sounds are used for the same purposes: to attract mates, scare away predators, or stop other bats from stealing their food. Bats' squeaks are too high-pitched for humans to hear. But zoologists—scientists who study animals—use special microphones to hear them.

Some bats are great at eavesdropping on their neighbors. If a bat is homing in on prey using echolocation, another bat might be listening in. The eavesdropper can then head toward the sound and scoop up any extra bugs that might be hanging around!

SAGE GROUSES

The greater sage grouse can be found in North America. Most of the time it makes cooing noises that sound similar to a pigeon, by passing air over its vocal cords. But when it's time to attract a mate, it produces a different noise that's sure to impress.

Under its beak, connected to its chest, the male sage grouse has two inflatable pouches called "gular sacs." When he wants to tell all the female grouse just how wonderful he is (and what an amazing dad he'll be) he uses the sacs to put on a real show. First he inflates the sacs with air so they stick out in front of him. Then he bobs his head forward and backward while shaking his tail feathers.

These booming pops, swishes, and whooshes sound a bit like the noise you make when you wobble a piece of metal. Together with flashes of their yellow sacs and broad tail feathers, the sage grouse's display certainly attracts attention!

BLACK-CAPPED CHICKADEES

Chickadees are small, social birds from the northern United States and Canada. These forest birds make a number of different high-pitched calls that help them reach other members of their flock.

HEEE-BEE!
(This is my territory!)

This regular high-pitched song is usually sung by males.

SQUE-KA-DEE
(Look at all this food!)

Chickadees get their name from the call they use to alert other chickadees to something—good or bad!

HEE-GRAG-PIP
(Hey!)

This "gargling" often means "don't get too close." It is used by high-ranking birds when talking to other members of the flock.

SQUE-KA-DEE-DEE-DEE-DEE-DEE-DEE
(Agh! Danger! Look out!)

If the number of "dees" in the call increases, it is likely that something more dangerous has been spotted.

HEEP-HEEP
(I'm still here, are you?)

These quiet cheeps are made by chickadees so that their buddies know where they are.

BIRDS OF PARADISE

More than 40 species of birds of paradise live in and around the huge island of New Guinea. The males are great dancers and strut their stuff in order to attract females. They all have different dances but they mean the same thing: "let's get together!"

The male superb bird of paradise flips his black wings over his head so that he forms an oval shape. He has a stripe of blue feathers that shines as he dances and hops around. He also makes clicking sounds.

The male greater bird of paradise has impressive plumes of long, yellow tail feathers. He will sit on a branch above a female and hop up and down on the branch while squawking to get her attention.

Male emperor birds of paradise also put on displays in the trees. They hang upside down from the branches to show off their strength and colors.

Male six-plumed birds of paradise (as shown here) start by tidying up their dance floor. They remove any stray leaves or twigs before opening their cape of feathers. They dance by moving from side to side and displaying their brightly colored neck feathers.

MIMICS

Some animals can be real copycats. A few clever species are able to imitate the calls, chatter and songs of other animals. Some birds are especially good at this. Parrots, for example, have an uncanny ability to mimic exactly what their owners say.

Lyrebirds are large, flightless Australian birds that are great impersonators. They can copy the calls of other species of birds as well as human-made sounds such as camera clicks and chainsaws. Their extremely complicated voice box (or syrinx) allows them to mimic almost any sound and turn it into part of their mating call.

Fork-tailed drongos use their mimicry to launch a clever assault and steal food from meerkats. Drongos and meerkats both enjoy munching on small insects, so the birds keep a lookout for when a meerkat has found a meal. By mimicking the warning sounds of meerkats, the birds can trick the meerkats into running for cover and dropping their food. While the meerkat scuttles away to safety, the bird swoops in and picks up a few tasty snacks. See how useful it can be to learn another animal's language?

RYAP!
(Let's get out of here!)

AUTHOR'S NOTE

By now you should be an expert in talking to some of the animals we share our planet with. Although the squeaks and grunts might take a bit of practice to get just right...

Writing this book was really fun, but I couldn't have done it without all the scientists who spend their careers studying their favorite species (more on that on the next page) and recording their sounds and behaviors.

Hopefully, now that you've read this book, you'll never feel tongue-tied when out in nature. If you ever find yourself face-to-face with a meerkat or in the water with a leaping dolphin, you might have a few phrases up your sleeve. But don't stop there—there's a world of sounds still to be discovered!

Many animals haven't yet been studied closely. And there are lots of sounds that we've heard but don't yet understand. Maybe you will be the next turkey translator or llama linguist...

Happy chatting!

Dr Nick

THE SCIENCE BEHIND THE SOUNDS

Learning an animal language is a lot like learning a new human language. You have to spend a long time listening to unfamiliar sounds before it starts to make sense.

Scientists who study animals are called zoologists. When investigating the ways that animals communicate they will often have to go into "the field" (which just means where animals live—sometimes that is an actual field, but not always!). The scientists have to be masters of disguise because they need to make sure that they aren't detected by the animals. If the animals know the scientists are there, they might change how they behave, which would ruin the experiment. Scientists need to record hours and hours of the animals' sounds. They then try to figure out which sounds are made at the same time as certain behaviors—like finding food, scaring away predators, or attracting a mate.

Another way scientists can figure out what some sounds mean is by playing recorded calls back to the animals through loudspeakers to see how they react. For example, if a call means "look out, danger!" all the animals will run

away when they hear it! Scientists can also use this method to find out which animals live in certain places. If they hear replies to the sound recordings, then they know that animals live there, even if they can't see them!

Some animal sounds—like bird calls—are easy to record, but others are more difficult. Scientists listening to animals that live in hard-to-reach places—like under the sea—have to use special microphones to hear their calls. For example, they might use hydrophones, which are special microphones that can be trailed underneath boats to listen to fish and whale sounds.

But scientists aren't just figuring out how to talk to our furry, feathered, or scaly neighbors. They are also trying to answer big, complicated questions. They might be figuring out how human-made noise pollution is affecting animal communication. Or how animals first evolved to talk to each other in the first place! It's amazing how one little squawk, squeak, or hiss can tell us so much about our world.

MEET THE AUTHOR

Dr. Nick Crumpton is a children's book writer and zoologist from London, UK. He wrote his first book for kids when he was finishing his PhD at the University of Cambridge and kept writing while working as a researcher for the BBC Natural History Unit. He now works at the Natural History Museum, London, where he is continually inspired by the amazing scientists who work there and the mind-blowing specimens kept behind the scenes. He loves hanging out with his partner's family collie Isla, and right now his favorite animals are sharks (although he might change his mind next week...).

MEET THE ILLUSTRATOR

Adrienne Barman was born in Ticino, Switzerland, and it was there that she first found a love of graphic design. She worked in Geneva as a freelance graphic designer and illustrator and then moved to Grandson, a small medieval Swiss town. Since 2006, she has produced about 30 illustrated books as well as comics for children and adults. Bright colors, the animal world, and offbeat nature are at the heart of her drawings. Her book *Creaturepedia* has been translated into 18 languages and won the 2015 Swiss Youth and Media Prize.

GLOSSARY

abdomen
The part of an animal that usually contains the gut. In insects, it is the section of the body farthest from the head.

aggressive
Describes very forceful behavior.

antennae
Parts of an insect's body that are string- or fan-like. They are found on the insect's head and are used for touch and smell.

backbone
A column of bone that supports the bodies of many animals, such as fish, amphibians, reptiles, birds, and mammals. Animals with a backbone are called vertebrates. The backbone is also called the spine.

biologist
A scientist who studies living things.

crustaceans
A group of invertebrates (animals that don't have a backbone) that includes crabs and lobsters.

dialect
A version of a language that is spoken in a particular location and uses some combination of words, pronunciation, and grammar that aren't used elsewhere.

echolocation
A method that some animals use to sense their surroundings by listening to the way that sounds echo off objects.

elegant
Describes something that is stylish and graceful.

entomologist
A scientist who studies insects.

gesture
The movement of a hand or other part of the body, often used in communication.

heart rate
The number of times a heart beats in a minute.

herbivore
An animal that only eats vegetation, such as leaves or other parts of plants.

imitate
Copy.

impersonator
A person or animal that copies the sounds or movements of another person or animal.

inflatable
Able to be made bigger by being filled with air or liquid.

intelligence
The ability to learn and understand information.

intimidate
Frighten or threaten.

intruder
Unwanted visitor.

invertebrates
Animals without backbones. Insects, octopuses, and most other animals are invertebrates.

knead
Lightly push down on something to stretch or soften it.

membrane
A thin layer of skin or other material.

mesmerize
To control someone's attention. Hypnotize.

mimic
Copy.

nocturnal
Active at night.

pheromones
Chemicals that animals release to send signals.

prattling
Meaningless, repetitive chatter.

predator
An animal that hunts and eats other animals.

prey
Animals that are eaten by other animals.

primates
Animals that belong to a group of mammals that includes lemurs, monkeys, and apes (including humans).

relatives
Members of a family.

reunited
Having met again after a time of being apart.

shock wave
High air pressure that is moving outward from an explosion.

social
Living as part of a community of other individuals.

solitary
Living alone.

species
A group of similar animals that are more closely related to each other than to other populations of animals. Species are grouped together by a name given to them by humans.

stallion
An adult male horse.

stridulation
A way of creating sound by rubbing parts of the body together quickly.

territorial
Having a specific area in which to hunt for food and look for mates, and not letting others use it.

territory
An area of land that is controlled by an animal or group of animals.

tranquil
Calm or quiet.

translation
Taking ideas heard in one language and speaking them in another language.

tymbals
Parts of a cicada's body that are used to make loud noises.

unpredictable
With an unknown future.

vocal cords
Parts of the body in the throats of some animals, including humans, that create sounds when air is pushed through.

zoologist
A scientist who studies animals.

INDEX

SELECTED SOURCES

Ackerman, Jennifer. *The Bird Way: A New Look at How Birds Talk, Work, Play, Parent, and Think* (Penguin Press, 2020, USA)

American Kennel Club www.akc.org

Attenborough, David. *Life of Birds* (BBC Books, 1998, UK)

Blue Planet II "Coral Reefs" [documentary] Narrated by Attenborough, David. (BBC, 2017)

Bradbury, J. W. and Vehrencamp, S. L. *Principles of Animal Communication* 2nd edition (Sinaeur, 2011, USA)

Britannica online www.britannica.com

Brumm, H. and Zollinger, S. A. "Vocal plasticity in a reptile" *Proc. R. Soc. B.* (2017)

Bura, V., Kawahara, A. and Yack, J. "A Comparative Analysis of Sonic Defences in Bombycoidea Caterpillars" in *Sci Rep* 6 (2016)

Chadwick, F., Fitzmaurice, B., Alton, S. and Earl, J. *The Bee Book* (Dorling Kindersley, 2016, UK)

Jézéquel, Y., Chauvaud, L. and Bonnel, J. "Spiny lobster sounds can be detectable over kilometres underwater" *Sci Rep* 10 (2020)

Krebs, J. R., Davies, N. B. (eds). *Behavioural Ecology: An Evolutionary Approach* (Blackwell Publishing, 1978, USA)

Life in Cold Blood "Land Invaders" [documentary] Narrated by Attenborough, David. (BBC, 2008)

"Naked Mole Rats 'Speak' Different Languages Just Like Us" www.youtube.com/watch?v=P2SdrOiHhtU

National Geographic "Overheard: Episode 1: Humpback whale song of the summer" www.nationalgeographic.com/podcasts/overheard/article/episode-1-humpback-whale-song

Practical Horseman www.practicalhorsemanmag.com

Scales, Helen. *Eye of the Shoal: A Fishwatcher's Guide to Life, the Ocean and Everything* (Bloomsbury Sigma, 2018, UK)

Sebeok, Thomas (ed). *How Animals Communicate* (Indiana University Press, 1978, USA)

Tavernier, C., Ahmed, S., Houpt, K. A. and Yeon, S. C. "Feline vocal communication" in *J Vet Sci.* (2020)

Yong, Ed. *An Immense World: How Animal Senses Reveal the Hidden Realms Around Us* (Vintage, 2022, UK)

HE EH EU EH
OUURF OUURF
RRRRARFF ARFF!
GRNNNT
AARK!
MEIOOW
GLP!
NEEEIGHEHEIHEI!
GRRRRRRRRR
MMWIA